Amish Proverbs

Words of Wisdom from the Simple Life

Suzanne Woods Fisher

Revell

a division of Baker Publishing Group
Grand Rapids, Michigan

© 2010 by Suzanne Woods Fisher

Published by Revell
a division of Baker Publishing Group
P.O. Box 6287, Grand Rapids, MI 49516-6287
www.revellbooks.com

Printed in China

Library of Congress Cataloging-in-Publication Data
Fisher, Suzanne Woods.
    Amish proverbs : words of wisdom from the simple life / Suzanne Woods Fisher.
       p.   cm.
    Includes bibliographical references.
    ISBN 978-0-8007-1953-1 (cloth)
    1. Conduct of life. 2. Amish—Conduct of life. 3. Aphorisms and apothegms. I. Title.
BJ1581.2.S553 2010
289.7'3—dc22   2009052931

To protect the privacy of those who have shared their stories with the author, some names and details have been changed.

10   11   12   13   14   15   16   7   6   5   4   3   2   1

To my mother, Barbara Benedict Woods,
who raised her children on Pennsylvania Dutch sayings.
This one is her favorite:
"Every mother crow thinks her own little crow is the blackest."

CONTENTS

CONTENTS

Acknowledgments

These collections are drawn, with permission, from a variety of sources: *The Sugarcreek Budget*, *Proverbs of the Pennsylvania Germans* by Dr. Edwin Miller Fogel, the *Pennsylvania German Dictionary* by C. Richard Beam, and the sayings and adages I grew up hearing from my grandfather's Old Order German Baptist Brethren family.

My grandfather—we called him Deardad—was famous for pointing out to me with a frown that "young folks should use their ears and not their mouths."

Another saying I grew up hearing was, "Choose your love and love your choice." That one belongs to my mother.

*If you want
to know a people,
know their proverbs.*

INTRODUCTION

THE AMISH IN THEIR OWN WORDS

Most every culture has proverbs that are unique to it. Whether called maxims, bromides, truisms, idioms, expressions, sayings, or just an old saw, proverbs are small, concentrated packages that let us peek into the window of a peoples' values and beliefs. They give us insight into a culture, its faith, folklore, history, language, mentality, psychology, worldview, and values. These pithy sayings are not meant to be universal truths. They contain general observations and experiences of humankind, including life's multifaceted contradictions.

"Proverbs," radio Bible teacher J. Vernon McGee once said, "are short sentences drawn from long experience."[1]

The ancient Eastern world—Egypt, Greece, China, and India—is thought to be the home of proverbs, dating back to collections from as early as 2500 BC. King Solomon, who reigned in the tenth century BC, gathered many of them from other sources as well as editing and authoring others. Over five hundred were compiled into the book of Proverbs in the Bible. Proverbs were used in monasteries to teach novices Latin. Often colorfully phrased, at times even musical in pronunciation, proverbs served as teaching tools for illiterate populations that relied on oral tradition.

Interestingly, the proverbs have played a surprisingly prominent role in the speech of the Pennsylvania Germans, which includes—though isn't limited to—the Amish. "It is natural that the Pennsylvania Germans should use the proverb extensively," writes Dr. Edwin Miller Fogel in his book *Proverbs of the Pennsylvania Germans* "because of the fondness of the Germanic peoples for this form of expression. The proverbs are the very bone and sinew of the dialect."[2]

"The ones that are common in the community are most likely in the oral tradition," says Dr. Donald B. Kraybill, senior fellow at the Young Center for Anabaptist and Pietist Studies at Elizabethtown College, Pennsylvania. "Not particularly Amish, but part of the broader rural tradition of the area."[3]

The Pennsylvania Deitsch dialect (which is called "Penn Dutch," though it has no relationship to Holland) originated in the Palatinate area of Germany over four hundred years ago and was brought to Pennsylvania in the 1700s with a wave of immigrants: Lutherans, Mennonites, Moravians, Amish, German Brethren, and German Reformed. Penn Dutch was, and is, an oral language; even today, people from different states can understand one another since the language has remained close to its origins.

"Most of what they [German immigrants] knew, they brought here from the Old World," explains C. Richard Beam, retired full professor of German at Millersville University. "The proverbs were an integral part of Pennsylvania German culture. The further back you go, the richer the language."

The cleverness of a proverb, though, can be lost in translation. Here's an example: *Wer gut Fuddert, daer gut Buddert.* "Good feed, much butter." Here's one that comes through a little smoother: *Bariye macht Sarige.* "Borrowing makes sorrowing."

Beam worries that the language has been watered down and diluted over this last century, as the external culture has crowded out its rich heritage. Raised in Pennsylvania, Beam says that all four of his grandparents spoke Deitsch as their first language. "We spent time with aunts and uncles and grandparents. That led to a richness of the culture, a preservation of the language. This was prior to radio and television." Beam is now 84 years old. "There's a saying I was raised with: 'Every time the sheep bleats, it loseth a mouthful.' That applies directly to the culture today." The dialect is losing words, he says. "Language doesn't stand still."

Today, only the Old Order Amish and the Old Order Mennonites have retained Deitsch as their first language. The Old Order Amish is a society that does not permit higher education. Theirs is a culture learned from the simplicity of their ancestor's lifestyles, and the Amish value this heritage. This simple lifestyle, passed virtually unchanged through the generations, provides an ideal base for the continual use of proverbs.

Within the last century, the use of proverbs in modern American society may have diminished, but not so for the Amish. In fact, the opposite is happening.

The Sugarcreek Budget is a weekly newspaper for the Amish-Mennonite community that began in 1890. Scribes from all over the world send in a weekly letter to the Ohio headquarters. At the end of most letters, a proverb is added, like a benediction. "The trend began about five to eight years ago," explains editor Fannie Erb-Miller. "We started to allow a saying on the end of a scribe's letter, and then it just caught on. Now, almost all of the letters have one. Early on, letters didn't include them. Mostly, they're sayings that pass from generation to generation. The proverbs are very relevant. They can speak to you. They can hit you."

The proverbs in this book, like all proverbs, come from many sources—most of them anonymous and all of them difficult to trace. It is not unusual to find the same proverb in many variants. The saying, "Bend the tree while it is young, when it is old, it is too late" is a variation on the Bible's "Train up a child in the way he should go: and when he is old, he will not depart from it" (Prov. 22:6 KJV).

God plays a prominent role in Amish proverbs, as does nature: weather and seasons, agriculture and animals. In our modern world, the rural savvy may seem outdated. But look a little deeper. The proverbs are every bit as relevant in the year 2010 as they were in 1710: *Der alt Bull blarrt als noch* means "The old bull keeps on bellowing," or to give it a twenty-first-century twist, "The old scandal will not die down."

These sayings and proverbs, dear to the Amish, can help the English (non-Amish) better understand them. For example, here are two proverbs that reveal how the Amish value the virtue of patience: "Only when a squirrel buries and forgets an acorn, can a new oak tree come forth," and "Adopt the pace of nature; her secret is patience."

Proverbs are just as useful in our life today as they are to Old Order Amish families. They're just as relevant to us as they were to the Israelites in King Solomon's day. They help point us toward wisdom, toward good judgment, toward God's teachings. To please God, we must know what he values: What does he care about? What does he love? What does he hate? Proverbs teach us about God.

That is the ultimate goal of the proverb: to help others learn by experience and live wisely, pleasing to God. By perpetuating these same phrases, we constantly remind ourselves of their importance and their power to prevent us from forgetting the lessons they hold.

One thing is certain: There is no such thing as a simple proverb.

Don't hurry, don't worry,
do your best, leave the rest!

TIME

Linda sat with her son in the emergency room
of their local hospital, waiting to be seen by a doctor.
Her son had twisted his ankle playing a game of basketball and
she worried he might have caused serious damage to it.

After ten minutes, her son grew fidgety and impatient. "This is going to
take forever," he moaned.

Seated across from them was a young Amish couple. The wife had taken
a spill and hurt her shoulder. They sat calmly, though Linda noticed the
wife wince in pain whenever she shifted in her seat. Finally, the nurse came
out and motioned to the Amish man. He jumped up to help his wife rise

to her feet. Linda heard him say to her, "Now, Katie, that wasn't too bad a wait. Only an hour."

After the Amish couple left the waiting room, Linda nudged her son with her elbow. "Do you see the difference? You expected to be seen immediately. They expected to wait."

To the Amish, waiting isn't a verb. It's an attitude. They wait for spring to plow and plant, for autumn to reap and harvest. They know that the seasons can't be rushed. They wait for the rain to come and nourish their crops. Much of their three-plus-hour church service is a time of silent waiting: they wait in expectation before God, rich with the promise of what is to come.

"Rest in the LORD, and wait patiently for Him" (Ps. 37:7 KJV) is a biblical principle the Amish take to heart. Waiting on the Lord is the same thing as trusting him. All that they have belongs to him, including the minutes and hours and days and years that make up their lives.

Time is just viewed differently for the Amish than for the English. It's not as important.

"In Indiana," says Dr. Joe Wittmer, raised in an Old Order Amish home, "the English move their clocks forward an hour in the spring and back an hour in the fall, but we never moved ours forward or back at any time. We went by 'sun' time and I don't remember being concerned about what time it was. Time was not important and we had only one clock in the house and it wasn't running most of the time. We based our time on 'sun up,' 'noon,' and 'dark' time."[1]

The Amish recognize patience as a key part of God's character. Conforming their will to God's will is what being Amish is all about. One way they try to conform is to purposefully slow down the tempo of life—an obvious example: they ride in a buggy pulled by a horse.

"We were never in a hurry," says Dr. Wittmer. "It's difficult to be in a hurry in a horse and buggy."

They have a deep connection to the rhythms of nature through their farm, even if it's just a few acres to grow their own fruits and vegetables. They eschew time thieves: television, radio, newspapers. It's as if they live their life with an unlimited amount of time, as if they have a toe in the door to eternity.

Common sayings promote patience as a virtue:

"It takes a century for God to make a sturdy oak."

"Harvest comes not every day."

"A handful of patience is worth more than a bushel of brains."

"You can't make cider without apples."

"Don't count your eggs before they are laid."

What a contrast to the English perception of time: there's never enough of it! Time is viewed as an enemy, or at the least, as an irritating constraint. We try to beat the clock, and use technology or machinery to speed up tasks. In an ironic twist, time seems even more elusive despite more gadgetry that promises us more spare time.

The Amish can teach us to slow down. Time is not something to be mastered, but a boundary to be respected. They remind us that Christians should look at life from a different perspective because we are part of a different kingdom—one that stretches into infinity.

"Run the race with eternity in view" and "What we do in this life echoes in eternity" are frequently quoted in sermons. And one thing the Amish know to be true: unlike humans, God is not in short supply of time. There is no limit to his days or his patience or his joy.

You may as well borrow a
person's money as his time.

———

Nothing lasts forever, not even your troubles.

———

You only live once,
but if you work it right, once is enough.

Many times we are climbing mountains
when we ought to be quietly resting.

Do more of less.

The years can fly past like a flock of birds.

One thing you can learn by watching the clock is that it passes time by keeping its hands busy.

Only one life, 'twill soon be past;
only what's done for Christ will last.

Patience is a virtue that carries a lot of wait.

In autumn sunshine, prepare for winter's cold.

A task takes as long as it takes.

———

Regrets over yesterday
and the fear of tomorrow are
twin thieves that rob us of the moment.

———

Enjoy today . . . it won't come back.

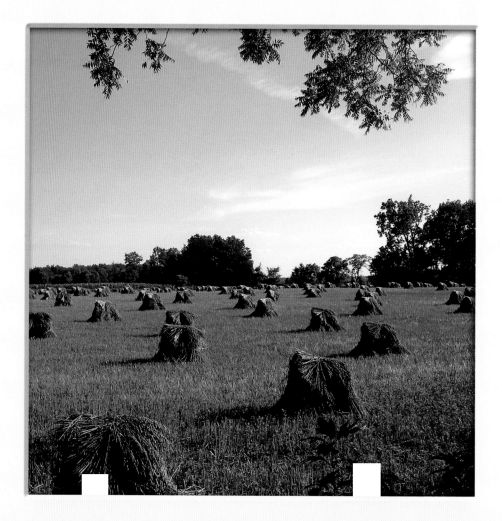

You can't make good hay from poor grass.

Live each short hour with God
and the long years will take care of themselves.

The years teach much which days never know.

Mutza
2.50

Those who have money
are troubled about it,
those who have none
are troubled without it.

MONEY

A few years ago, I called an Old Order Amish farm in Pennsylvania to make a reservation to stay for a trip I had planned. I left a message on an answering machine and received a return call just a few hours later from a woman named Viola Stoltzfus. Viola called from the phone shack down the lane from her farm. Every few minutes, her gentle voice—with just a trace of an accent—was drowned out by the clip-clop sounds of a horse and buggy passing by. After Viola wrote down the dates of my visit, I asked her how much money I should send to reserve the room.

"Well," she said, "we're too busy to make a breakfast for you. So, just send me a donation."

Nonplussed, I had absolutely no idea how much to send, so I wrote out a check for the amount I was spending at an airport hotel the night before. As I sealed that envelope to Viola and stuck a stamp on it, I couldn't remember ever feeling so good about writing someone a check. Why? Viola offered me two things that are in short supply in a secular world: She wasn't trying to unduly profit off of my visit but to receive a fair exchange for goods and services. And she trusted me to decide what that would be worth.

"As the work, so the pay," goes the saying.

It's not that the Amish aren't money savvy; they are. But their goal in life isn't to accumulate wealth. Money is a tool, not a goal. They want only to support their family in an environment that best reflects their values. They believe in ownership of land, hard work, frugality, honesty, and industry. But they strive to prevent affluent living, keeping up with the Joneses, and social status. In fact, they don't even value the indicators of success that we prize: income, education, luxuries, and symbols of prosperity. To the Amish way of thinking, "If fools have much, they spend much."

Many proverbs warn of the dangerous effects of affluence: corruption, laziness, friendlessness. Suspicion surrounds wealth. Many proverbs reflect this mistrust:

"The rich are poor payers."

"Where there's money, you'll find the devil."

"A full purse never lacks friends."

Instead, the Amish give their highest respect to those who care well for their homes and families and community, those who raise their children so they will grow up wanting to become Amish, and those who help the next generation settle on farms. "It is a wealthy person, indeed, who calculates riches not in gold but in friends."

The Amish put the brakes on accumulation and all of the distractions and complications that come with it. There's a point where enough is enough, especially if it interferes with what is truly important to them: faith, family, community. That's where they draw the line.

Enough is enough is a rare concept for our modern world. A curious finding by a 2009 study shines a spotlight on one result of affluence: the higher the income, the less time a family spends together. [1] The decline in family time, the study found, coincided with a rise in Internet use and the popularity of social networks. Whether it's around the dinner table or just in front of the TV, the study found that American families are spending less time together.

The Amish remind us that there is goodness and satisfaction in a simpler life.

Where is your line drawn? When is enough, enough?

Those who let God provide
will always be satisfied.

A person may hoard up money, he may bury
his talents, but you cannot hoard up love.

Money talks, but it doesn't say
when it's coming back.

You get what you pay for.

You are only poor when you
want more than you have.

He who has no money is poor; he who
has nothing but money is even poorer.

The debt that is paid is best.

If you're careful with your pennies, the dollars will take care of themselves.

A dollar saved is a dollar earned, but seldom vice versa.

A full purse never lacks friends.

Laziness travels so slowly that
poverty soon overtakes it.

———

Fortune knocks once but misfortune
has more patience.

———

Thoughts are tax-free.

An industrious wife is the best savings account.

⁓⊹⊹⊹⁓

Generosity leaves a much better
taste than stinginess.

⁓⊹⊹⊹⁓

A man is rich in proportion to the
things he can afford to leave alone.

↓13FT 3IN↓

A happy life and eternal salvation is spoiling the devil's calculation.

FAITH

Mary Miller is a thin, attractive Amish woman of 46, a mother to eight children born within a span of eleven years. During the day, Mary wears a starched white organza prayer cap over her tightly pinned hair bun. In the night, she wears another covering. Why does she wear a head covering at night? "In case I wake up in the night and need to pray," Mary explains in a tone that suggests it should be quite obvious. "And with eight children, I do. Often."

Religion is 24/7 for the Amish. Everything they do, especially the manner in which they dress, is based upon their faith. Their simple clothing—a tradition of the Amish and the reason they are also called the Plain People—is a tangible reminder that they are a people set apart, belonging to the

Lord. The *Kapp* or "head cap," worn by every woman and even by infants, might be the most symbolic garment of all. As girls become young teens, they start to wear the cap: black for Sunday dress and a white cap at home. After marriage a white cap is always worn. The style and size of caps can vary among church districts, but it is essentially the same cap as that worn by the Palatine women of the seventeenth and eighteenth centuries. Back in those days, the Amish were perceived as radicals.

To a modern world, the Amish still seem radical. Their deep commitment to faith is why they choose to live separate from the world. They believe the ways of the world oppose God. They eschew accumulating materialistic goods because it leads them to pride. Their Plain clothes serve to keep them separate from the world by creating a unifying identity. Their dependence on a caring community is intended to reflect the body of Christ. Their emphasis on humility reminds them that God alone is worthy of praise. Try to pay an Amish person a sincere compliment and you will most likely get a soft-spoken deflection in return: "Oh, I don't know about that."

The Amish take temptation to pride very seriously. "Because of our tendency toward pride," says David Miller, Mary's husband, "we need the cross, the Spirit, and the example of Christ." The Lord's Prayer holds great meaning to the Amish and in it Christ's petition: "Lead us not into temptation, but deliver us from evil."

Many proverbs warn of pride that leads to disaster:

"The crowing hen comes to no good end" is pretty clear.

"Nothing in front and nothing behind" means a person is proud and has nothing to be proud of.

David has made a lifelong practice of memorizing Scripture. He likens the Scriptures to "plumb bobs"—the weight that always holds a builder's plumb line straight and true. David seeks to measure his own thoughts, feelings, and behavior by God's Word—regardless of the circumstances. "Standing your ground is easier," he says, "when you are grounded in God's Word."

Most Amish believe the adage that, "The cornerstone of faith is truth, not tolerance." They take Scripture literally and don't rationalize or justify behaviors that the Bible labels as sin. Evil is evil, and the source of evil is the devil, for whom they have a healthy respect. Traditional sayings make the devil sound active and nearly ever-present:

"Speak of the devil and you'll hear the flop of his wings."

"You need not call the devil, he'll come without calling."

And no one is immune to temptation: "Even a saint is tempted by an open door."

But the focus of the Amish life is not solely on avoiding temptation. It is on pleasing God, conforming to his will, living a faithful life, and hoping for an eternity in his presence. After all, to their way of thinking, "The best way to escape evil is to pursue good."

Bibles that are coming apart
usually belong to people who are not.

It may be difficult to wait on the Lord,
but it is worse to wish you had.

He who bows lowest in the presence of God
stands straightest in the presence of sin.

Faith is the bridge over which we can cross
all the unknown waters of tomorrow.

In creation, God spoke and it was so.
He used his finger to deal with the devil and
he made bare his mighty arm to save us.

You can't stumble when you are on your knees.

God speaks to those who are quiet before him.

The higher a man gets in divine grace,
the lower he will be in his own esteem.

A heart at peace gives life to the body.

When fear knocks at the door,
send faith to answer!

Doubt has never changed anything.
Belief changes things.

Walk softly, speak tenderly,
and pray fervently.

*Let your life story
be for God's glory.*

When you get to your wit's end,
you'll find God lives there.

When I have nothing left but God,
then I find that God is all I need.

We are never worthless, but unworthy.

Faith produces a way of life that pleases God.

If you want your life to be
a reflection of Christ, you need to
take time to reflect on Christ.

A faith worth having
is a faith worth sharing.

If you sense your faith is unraveling, go back
to where you dropped the thread of obedience.

Faith hears the inaudible,
sees the invisible, believes the incredible,
and receives the impossible.

Faith gives us the courage to
face the present with confidence
and the future with expectancy.

Don't pray when it rains,
if you don't pray when the sun shines.

Be faithful and leave the results to God.

If you are true to your faith,
there are things you give up for your faith.

We should not put a question mark
where God puts a period.

Wherever we go, God is there.
Whenever we call, God is listening.
Whatever we need, God is enough.

Every moment of worry
weakens the soul for its daily combat.

When you find time on your hands,
put them together in prayer.

Know the Bible in your head,
stow it in your heart,
show it in your life,
sow it in the world.

A child can read
a parent's character
before he can read
the alphabet.

Children & Family

In the Old Order Amish district in Indiana where Joe Wittmer was raised, the birth of a baby was greeted with love, joy and "sweet coffee."

"*Siess Kaffi*," says Dr. Wittmer, "is what neighbors do when a new baby arrives. The mom is given a week or so to rest, then folks start coming by with a meal and to see the new baby. They all have 'sugar in their coffee.'"

Some say there is no better babyhood than that enjoyed by an Amish baby. The Amish baby is an integral part of the family from the moment of birth. Even when asleep, the infant is often held in someone's arms. The Amish rarely, if ever, use babysitters. It's customary to take the baby with them wherever the parents go, even to long church services.

Dr. Wittmer says he's never known of a time when the birth of a child is an unwelcomed event. "A baby means another corn husker, another cow-milker, but most of all, another God-fearing Amishman. The birth is always seen as a blessing of the Lord."

Children are considered a gift from God and family size attests to that: the average Amish family has seven children. Parents practice no birth control and pray for children. With such a high birthrate, the Amish have become the fastest growing population in the United States. As of 2009, the Young Center for Anabaptist and Pietist Studies at Elizabethtown College in Pennsylvania calculated there are over 233,000 Amish.[1] Over half the population is under eighteen years of age.

"Children are the poor man's wealth," says one proverb.

If faith is the cornerstone of Amish society, the home is the foundation. Marriage among the Amish is highly esteemed and raising a family is like a professional career for adults. Divorce is virtually unheard of. One father wrote in *Family Life* magazine, "Children have only one childhood. We can fail in business and often times start over and make good. But if we fail in the teaching and training of our children, we never get another chance."

Being family-centered is a long held and deeply cherished Amish standard. "I can't put into words all that a home means to the Amish," says Dr. Wittmer. "It's almost something too deep for words. Family is number one." While in his *Rumspringa* (a term used for adolescence that is translated as "running around"), Joe Wittmer found the game of basketball. He went to high school, then to college. "I didn't go to get an education but to play basketball," he says. "I always had a plan to go back." But the path he started on led him to graduate school where he eventually earned a doctorate in counseling psychology.

Does he regret leaving his heritage? "Would I trade? No. But I've always had that void."

Dr. Wittmer remains in close touch with his family. He was never baptized as a church member, thus he was not excommunicated. Today, he lives in Florida, but when he returns to Indiana, a large family reunion is held for him. "Over one hundred people," he says with a grin. "Everyone brings a dish. They all come."

Amish roots are strong, much more so than in contemporary American families. Many Amish live within several miles of their childhood homes. A typical Amish child may have two dozen aunts and uncles living in the area, plus dozens of cousins. Extended families are a blessing to each other and often live on the same piece of land.

"Youth likes to play, and old age to scold" sounds like something the middle-aged generation might mutter under their breath after a long day.

Sharing concern for a child's upbringing is a chief benefit of growing up in a thick network of extended family. "Parents and grandparents," says Laura

Mast, an elderly Amish woman with fifty-two grandchildren and counting, "have the biggest job in the world. We have to teach the young to love the Lord." Properly raised children ensure a bright future for the Amish. These children will one day provide a home for their aging parents, as Laura's son and daughter-in-law are now doing for her.

What's Laura's best child rearing advice? She answers with these proverbs: "Children need models more than critics" and "Children live what they learn and learn what they live." Another, she says, is, "Always treat children in the direction you wish them to grow, not as they now are."

But even more important than providing an Amish-style social security, parents' greatest desire for their children is to share their hope for a heaven-bound future. One proverb that Erik Wesner, author of the popular blog *Amish America,* often hears is: "Our children are the only treasures we can take to heaven."

A house is made of walls and beams;
a home is made of love and dreams.

A sweater is a garment worn by a child
when his mother feels chilly.

A wife will make or break a household.

Parents who are afraid to put their foot down
usually have children who step on their toes.

Children are the living messages we send
to a time we will not see.

Summer is the season when children
slam the doors they left open all winter.

Put the swing where the children want it.
The grass will grow back.

A father ought to help his son to form
the habit of doing right on his own initiative
rather than out of fear of serious consequences.

More is caught than taught.

Raising boys is as easy as digesting iron.

If you let your children have their own way,
you must not complain if they give you trouble.

Teaching children to count is fine,
but teaching them what counts is better.

The most important things in
your home are people.

Keep your feet under your own table.

If parents don't train their children,
the children will train the parents.

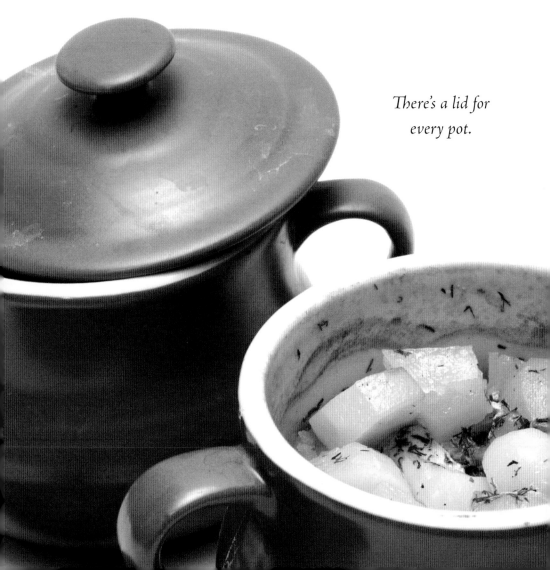

There's a lid for every pot.

*The person who thinks too little
usually talks too much.*

In Word & Deed

Edna is a soft spoken, gracious woman in her nineties. Born and raised in Ohio, she was the eldest in a large Amish family. "I never heard my parents use the words 'I love you,'" she says. "But I knew they did. It just wasn't the Plain way. It wasn't until I married [a non-Amish man] that I started to use those words. It was difficult at first, even to tell my own children I loved them." She looks up. "But I think they knew that I did."

Her daughter, Judy, is by her side, bobbing her head in agreement. "We knew, Mom."

A theme in Amish life is to live by example, not by words. Expressions of sentiment are rare, not necessarily because they don't have deep feelings, but because it seems worldly to air one's emotions. Words are not cheap to the Amish. "Where water is deepest it is stillest" best sums it up.

Threaded throughout many Amish sayings is a great emphasis on filtering one's speech: "You can't hang a man for his thoughts, but you mustn't think too loud." Careless talk and gossip are frowned upon. "Think ten times, talk once," or "What one is ashamed to do one should be ashamed to say." Or here's one that makes you wonder about who coined it and why: "A woman's tongue is the last thing about her that dies."

To the Amish, how a person acts says more about their faith than what they say they believe. The lack of emphasis Plain People place on evangelism is often misunderstood. Setting an example of a holy life, they feel, makes a better witness than mere talk. Rather than proselytize, the Amish provide practical help when natural disasters strike.

For example, busloads of young Amish men from the Lancaster area traveled to Pass Christian, Mississippi, to help rebuild homes after Hurricane Katrina. To their way of thinking, "You can preach a better sermon with your life than with your lips."

The messages behind "Actions speak louder than words" or "Kind actions begin with kind thoughts" seem so ordinary that we almost pass them by—but we shouldn't. Think of the impact of a good deed or a kind word. "Good deeds have echoes."

There's a biblical proverb behind this way of thinking: "Your own soul is nourished when you are kind; it is destroyed when you are cruel" (Prov. 11:17 LB). What is a nourished soul? It's one that feels inner joy and peace. Not smugness or pride or self-righteousness, but a deep down awareness that you are doing the work of God. The Amish believe that we are made in the image of a God who is by nature *good*. Doing good *is* God's work.

To quote an Amish scribe in *The Budget*: "Do all the good you can, by all the means you can, in all the ways you can, in all the places you can, at all the times you can, to all the people you can, as long as you can."[1]

A fault mender is better than a fault finder.

An unkind remark is like a killing frost—
no matter how much it warms up,
the damage is already done.

A smile is a curve that can
straighten out a lot of things.

All that you do, do with your might.
Things done by halves are never done right.

Swallowing words before you say them
is so much better than having
to eat them afterward.

When you speak, always remember
that God is one of your listeners.

To mistreat God's creation is
to offend the Creator.

⁕

Blessed are they who have nothing to say,
and who cannot be persuaded to say it.

⁕

Your actions speak so loudly
I can't hear a word you say.

We live simply so others may simply live.

In general those who have nothing to say
contrive to spend the longest time in doing it.

The smallest deed is better than
the greatest intention.

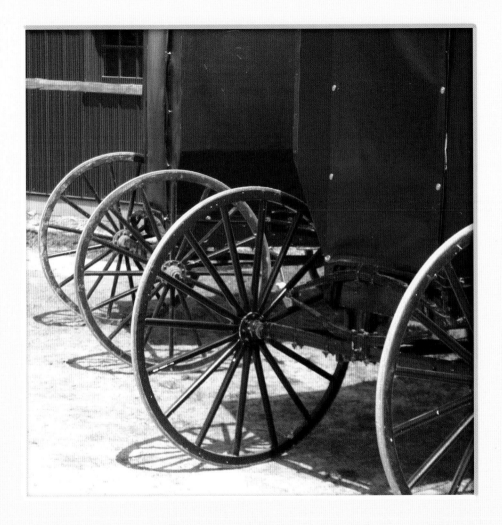

It is easier to preach a sermon
than to live one.

Even though you can hide from the earth, heaven sees you act.

———

Cut *h* off of "habit" and you will have "a bit" left. Cut off *a* and you still have a "bit." Cut off *bit* and you will have "it" conquered.

———

Why is it so hard to say "I broke it" and so easy to say "it broke"?

Kind words and kind deeds
keep life's garden free of weeds.

***

It takes 73 muscles to frown and
only 14 to smile. No wonder grouchy
people are always tired.

***

To overcome sin, starve the old
nature and feed the new.

A person who gets all wrapped up in himself makes a mighty small package.

———

He talked much but said little.

———

Anger makes your mouth work faster than your mind.

———

Three are too many to keep a secret.

A good name, like good will,
is earned by many actions
and lost by one.

Work Ethic

The Washington Post ran a story about a woman in southern Maryland who wanted to have a modular house built.[1] She asked friends and relatives for a recommendation for a good contractor. She finally settled on one: an Amish builder with an excellent reputation. She drove out to the builder's farm (since he was Amish, he had no phone) and described to him the kind of house she wanted. Happily, she agreed to the price tag he gave her, far lower than she had expected. In fact, commercial builders had quoted two to three times the price of the Amish builder.

But there were two parts of the arrangement that shocked her. One was the builder's waiting list: two years. The other was that there was no contract, no deposit required. Only a handshake to seal the deal. The transaction was based on trust.

If there is one characteristic the Amish are admired for, it is their strong work ethic. The Amish brand sells. It's even become a source of controversy as non-Amish businesses try to capitalize on the brand by labeling their products as Amish ones. "A general rule of thumb," says Erik Wesner, a scholar who studies the Amish and runs the *Amish America* blog, "is that if it *says* Amish, then it ain't."

Instilling a work ethic starts at a young age. Teaching a child to work and accept responsibility is one of the most important traits Amish parents hope to instill in their children. Traditional sayings strongly emphasize the renowned Amish work ethic:

"He that cometh first to the mill, grindeth first."

"The morning hour has gold in hand, woe to those who heed it not."

Perseverance is encouraged: "If you don't give up you haven't lost."

An Amish child begins "choring" at the age of four or five and the care of farm animals plays a big role in teaching daily responsibility. Boys and girls learn to feed chickens, gather eggs, and bottle nurse the calf. At a later age, most children are given charge of an animal—usually a calf or heifer—that will become exclusively theirs. The fate of the animal is linked to the care and attention it is given. The child learns the direct consequences of feeding, growth, birth, breeding . . . or neglect and disease. And in the natural course of events, they learn about death too. "He cares more about the wool than he does about the sheep" is an insult. It says that how an individual treats animals can unmask the truth about his character to others.

After Amish teenagers leave school at eighth grade and begin working, they customarily give their paychecks to their parents until they marry or turn 21. Parents provide a small allowance and bank the remainder. When a child marries, most parents will then help with the purchase of a farm or the start-up of a business. Amish parents believe that too much money at too young an age only leads to temptations. "Give the child a finger and he will want the whole hand" is an old-fashioned way of saying that providing too much can de-motivate a child. Here's another one: "Give a child his will, and a whelp his fill, and neither will thrive."

Laziness ranks as a cardinal sin. "Yes, tomorrow and not today, is what all lazy people say." "A lazy donkey will work itself to death sooner than a busy one" is another way of saying that laziness kills quicker than activity. "A lazy sheep thinks its wool heavy" is a person who can't take care of their own obligations.

Let's turn this around. While laziness is a disgrace, working hard—with integrity and honesty—are cherished characteristics, even if these qualities cause a person to be taken advantage of by others. The Amish live by the proverbs, "It is better to suffer wrong than to commit wrong" and "A man is happier to be sometimes cheated than to never trust." If they are wronged, so be it. They will not fight in wars. They will not sue anyone in a court of law. To the Amish way of thinking, vengeance belongs to God. They conduct modern business the old-fashioned way—with a handshake, a word of honor, and trust.

A truly happy person is one who can enjoy the scenery of a detour.

***

Advice when most needed is least heeded.

***

Those who can't forget are worse than those who can't remember.

A heart at peace gives life to the body.

Those who fear the future
are likely to fumble the present.

Encouragement is oxygen to the soul.

The soundness of your ideas is more important than the sound of your words.

Don't believe everything you think!

It is better to give others a piece of your heart than a piece of your mind.

The key to contentment
is to realize life is a gift—not a right.

A man should not grieve overmuch,
for that is a complaint against God.

If you think you're too small to
make a difference, you haven't
been in bed with a mosquito.

Contentment is not getting what we want
but being satisfied with what we have.

People who reject law and order
change their minds when they can
lay down the laws and give the orders.

If you put your finger to the fire,
it will get burned.

If we live right each day, we need neither be afraid of tomorrow or ashamed of yesterday.

You don't need to get sick to get better.

God's best is known by surrender—not struggle.

Contentment and trust are
characteristics of a sanctified life.

If we don't stand for something,
we will fall for anything.

Some people never learn anything
because they understand everything too soon.

If you can't see the bright side,
polish the dull.

The reason some people get lost in thought
is because it is unfamiliar territory.

Peace is rarely denied to the peaceful.

God has work for all his children,
regardless of age or ability.

God has two dwellings, one in heaven and
the other in a meek and thankful heart.

You cannot be truly a son of God
without resembling the Father.

The secret to getting ahead is getting started.

The trouble with doing nothing is
it's too hard to tell when you're finished.

Pride in your work
puts joy in your day.

Happiness doesn't come from doing what we like to do, but liking what we have to do.

———————

There is no limit to what a man can do if he doesn't care who gets the credit.

The one thing that is worse than a quitter
is the man who is afraid to begin.

If you want life's best,
see to it that life gets your best.

Do you know what happens when you give
a procrastinator a good idea? Nothing!

The higher the mountain,
the deeper the valley.

Handling Adversity

In late November 2008, Daniel Troyer was told by his doctors that he needed surgery to repair a valve in his heart. The surgery took place a few weeks later. The very next morning, an icy and cold December day, Daniel's eight year-old grandson was hit by a car as he walked to school. He was killed instantly.

Later that week, still recovering, Daniel was able to attend his grandson's funeral. The Old Order Amish bishop concluded the service by saying not once, not twice, but three times: "God always has a plan."

The Amish believe that God is sovereign over this world—everyone and everything in it. "Adversity is just part of life and you cope with adversity by accepting it," says Dr. Joe Wittmer, author of *The Gentle People*:

An Inside View of Amish Life. Such yielding to God's will is a distinctive Amish trait.

Non-Amish Christians typically (maybe not accurately, but typically) believe that their faith will deliver them *from* adversity. The Amish believe they will be delivered *in* adversity. When bad things happen, they don't question if God exists or why he would allow such a thing. "That does not mean that they do not grieve a death, for example, but their grief always seems lighter to me," says Dr. Wittmer. "Maybe because it is shared by the entire community. An individual really has no control over adversity or much of anything else, for that matter."

A traditional saying that means no one can tell what a day may bring forth is: "Hale at morn and dead by night."

Rather than question God's ways—which the Amish would perceive as prideful—they strengthen their faith by dwelling on God's character and the hope for eternity. Notice in these sayings how the focus is on God's provision to endure a difficult circumstance:

"God is there to give us strength for every hill we have to climb."

"Never doubt in the dark what God has shown you in the light."

"Trusting God turns problems into opportunities."

The Amish are no strangers to adversity. They are descendants of European Anabaptists, who in the late sixteenth century were the radicals of the day, persecuted and martyred for their beliefs. A secret police force of "Anabaptist hunters" was organized to spy on, locate, and arrest Anabaptists for their nonconformist beliefs. The Amish found refuge in remote parts of France, Switzerland, and Germany, and farmed land that no one else wanted. Even today, at every church service, they sing centuries' old hymns that recall those days of persecution.

With such a background of hardships, self-sufficiency became a core value for the Amish. Today they don't purchase insurance policies, they don't accept any government subsidies or pensions (though they do pay taxes), they don't send their children to public school.

"It's your own fault, if you leave the table hungry" or "When the cover is short, you must pull up your legs" reflect the attitude that the Amish don't expect this world to cater to them. In a matter-of-fact way, they expect the rain to fall on the just and the unjust: "This is the way of the world, one has the stockings, the other the shoes."

But the Amish do take care of their own. Mutual aid is provided to help in times of medical or financial difficulties. The barn raising might be the best metaphor to illustrate how the Amish handle adversity. When a barn burns down, they don't dwell on why it burned, they gather together to rebuild. And then they praise God: for the lumber, the nails, the caring community that skillfully puts it together, the animals that will inhabit it, and for a chance to start again.

God won't lead you
where his grace can't keep you.

If you find a pathway with no obstacles,
it probably doesn't lead anywhere.

Hope for the best, prepare for the worst,
and take what comes with a smile.

The best way to escape from a
problem is to solve it.

Nothing is all wrong: even a clock that has
stopped running is right twice a day.

Someday the scales of justice
will be perfectly balanced.

There are lots of ways to cut a cake.

⁂

Learn from your failures,
or you will fail to learn.

⁂

The best way to escape evil is to pursue good.

Just when the caterpillar thought the
world was over, it became a butterfly.

There's only one way to fail, that's to quit.

We value the light more fully
after we've come through the darkness.

God could save us from trauma,
but instead he sends us a Comforter.

If you get to the end of the rope,
tie a knot and hang on.

Instead of complaining
that the rosebush is full of thorns,
be glad that the thornbush has roses.

Life can be compared to rowing across a swift stream. We must continue our efforts of paddling against the current, or we shall drift downstream to the rocks and rapids and not reach the other shore.

All the water in the world cannot sink our boat as long as it's on the outside.

Life is a grindstone. Whether it grinds you down or polishes you up depends upon what you are made of.

Be like the teakettle;
when it's up to its neck
in hot water, it sings.

You can tell when
you're on the right track.
It's usually uphill.

*No man is his craft's
master the first day.*

EDUCATION

Naomi Weaver grew up in Holmes County, Ohio in a large Amish family. In September of 1962, as the new school year started up, Naomi's father decided she had enough public schooling and kept her home. Her birthday was in the fall, anyway. So what's a month or two?

The truant officer held a different point of view. He paid a visit to Naomi's home with a police officer and had her father arrested. Naomi's father spent a day in the county jail.

"After that," Naomi said, "I went to school every day! Until I turned sixteen. Then, happily, I quit." Naomi laughed at the memory but admitted it wasn't so funny when her dad was taken away in a police car.

Although the Amish are peaceable people, they can be surprisingly stubborn. There are some areas that they will not budge on. Take, for example, higher education. "Rub up against a black kettle and you will become black" summarizes the Amish view of public education.

For the first half of the twentieth century, Amish children attended public schools. For most of rural America, that consisted of one-room schoolhouses. Under local control, these schools posed little threat to Amish values. But the massive consolidation of public schools after World War II sparked clashes between the Amish and state officials—such as the one Naomi's dad faced. After legal skirmishes in several states, the U.S. Supreme Court gave the green light to the eighth-grade Amish school system in 1972, permitting Amish youth to complete formal schooling at the age of fourteen.

Small, parochial schools are critically important to the Amish; they help preserve the culture by reinforcing values and insulating "scholars" from contaminating worldly ideas. These one-room schools prepare children for meaningful lives in Amish society by teaching cooperation, responsibility, hard work, and basic skills for living. Their goal is to support Amish ways.

"If education is to be judged by its achievements, the Amish may have one of the most effective instructional systems in the world today," writes Dr. Joe Wittmer.[1]

Though the classroom work ends at the eighth grade, an Amish education carries on at home. Children continue to learn trades and homemaking skills, all steeped in the same ethics of working hard and responsibly. In fact, much of the Amish educational process takes place at home. Amish parents believe it is their obligation—not the state's—to educate their children. School and church are an extension of home; however, the chief models of the Amish culture are Mom and Dad.

The Amish have a suspicion about higher education. "He knoweth much who knows that he knows nothing" or "He who knows least hast most to say" or "Those who hold their heads too high haven't much in 'em" reflect a disdain for the pridefulness that the Amish believe often accompanies higher education.

Don't misunderstand. The Amish highly regard learning—but not for its own sake. Education is purposeful, and experience makes for the best teacher. "Experience keeps a dear school but fools learn in no other," one proverb explains. The Amish value learning by doing and are remarkably adept at finding specific information to learn a new skill. Because they have no exposure to other media, the Amish spend much more time reading than most Americans. Illiteracy is virtually nonexistent.

"Being lifelong learners is very important to them," says Dr. Wittmer. "They have to learn new skills all the time. They've learned how to work hard since they were young children. They've gotten up in the cold with a lantern to milk the cows at 4 a.m. That's the way they've done it, they still work hard. They apply that same work ethic to learning new skills."

Walnut Creek, Ohio, is home to Carlisle Press, a small Amish-run printing company. The owner adds this message to the back of each book: "Marvin Wengerd is a member of the Amish and he represents one of the many young Amish entrepreneurs who are developing new businesses apart from farming while at the same time remaining faithful to their Amish traditions. He and the employees of his company are dedicated to producing a quality product for their customers. They are mostly self-taught in the printing business and continue to expand their knowledge about printing."

Learning, for the Amish, is not attached to a report card or SATs or getting into the right college. Learning is attached to life.

Knowledge is the power of the mind.
Wisdom is the power of the soul.

Young folks should use their ears
and not their mouths.

Learning is far more valuable than education.

Some read just enough to keep
themselves misinformed.

It's what you learn after you
know it all that counts.

⸻

Remember, when you talk,
you only repeat what you already know;
if you listen, you might learn something.

One can learn something new every day.

It ain't the things you don't know
what gets you into troubles;
it's the thing you know for sure
that ain't so.

Knowledge is power, but like power,
it must be hitched to something effective.

A man cannot be robbed of his learning.

The only time to look down on your neighbor
is when you're bending over to help.

COMMUNITY

When Judy, a sixty-something woman with salt-and-pepper hair, was diagnosed with breast cancer, she faced a rigorous schedule of surgery and radiation. Her husband, friends, and neighbors were with her each step of the way. Her husband attended every doctor's appointment and kept a notebook filled with detailed notes of what the doctor said, so they could refer back to it at home. Her friends brought meals after the surgery and on radiation days, and prayed daily for her recovery.

"Having everyone's support and practical help felt like the warm blanket you get wrapped up with after surgery," says Judy. "The circumstances of having cancer hadn't changed, but the love and care of others helped me get through it."

People need people. Everyone needs a community. Isn't that what is behind the exploding success of social networks such as Facebook and Twitter? People seeking people. We have a longing to be needed and to belong to something bigger than ourselves. It's just the way God wired us. The sayings, "No one is strong enough to bear his burdens alone" and "Compassion puts love into action" reflect Judy's experience.

Most people think of community as a place, a geographical location. In reality—for Amish or non-Amish—communities are much more than a physical place. They are the world where people live, work, raise their children, and go to church.

Community is an extremely important aspect of Amish life because the Amish's religious values emphasize the importance of living together as a body of believers. It's one of the reasons the Amish remain tied to the horse and buggy—it creates an invisible boundary. They need to live in close proximity to each other to maintain face-to-face contact with family, friends, and neighbors. Even the size of the church district is kept intentionally small so that all members are within one hour's ride of each other. When a church district gets too large to accommodate members in a home [the Amish worship in homes], it will divide into two.

The Amish world revolves around a local turf. The same people frequently work, play, and worship together. They join together to help raise a barn, to sew a quilt, to build a new schoolhouse, and then to maintain it.

"After a threshing frolic [a work party to help a farmer thresh his crop]," says Dr. Joe Wittmer, who was raised in an Old Order Amish home, "we'd have a thresher meeting to settle up. If one farmer had help for three days and another for four, he'd pay up for that extra person. It was a time of celebration, that the crops were in. And we'd always have homemade ice cream."

With each event, Amish people attach more deeply as a community, belonging in a way beyond measure. Such is the saying, "People with a heart for God have a heart for people."

The Amish live together, worship together, socialize together. They help each other—as friends, neighbors, relatives, all members of a church district. Community, for the Amish, is not made from a place. Community is made up of familiar faces and helping hands.

Love enables us to walk fearlessly,
to run confidently, and to live victoriously.

Community is like an old coat—
you aren't aware of it until it is taken away.

The best vitamin for making friends is B1.

It is better to hold out a helping hand
than to point a finger.

We cannot catch our neighbor's foxes.

Two cannot quarrel when one will not.

Tackle the problem, not the person.

Cheerfulness greases the axles of the world.

A small leak will sink a large ship.

Too many people limit their exercise to jumping to conclusions, running up bills, stretching the truth, bending over backwards, lying down on the job, sidestepping responsibility, and pushing their luck.

Be kind to unkind people.
They probably need kindness the most.

Develop a forgiving attitude.

We can stop forgiving others
when Christ stops forgiving us.

Our duty is not to see through one another,
but to see one another through.

If you listen through the wall,
you'll hear others reciting your faults.

Details beget more details.

Love always finds a home
in the heart of a friend.

The waves of hatred beat in vain
against the rock of love.

When it comes to doing things for others,
some people stop at nothing.

We need old friends to help us grow old
and new friends to help us stay young.

***

Mentioning the faults of others
does not rid us of our own.

***

There is no greater love
than the love that holds on where there
seems nothing left to hold on to.

Kind words can be short and easy to speak
but their echoes are truly endless.

———— ◦◦◦◦ ————

We always admire the other fellow more
after we have tried to do his job.

———— ◦◦◦◦ ————

Before you flare up at anyone's faults,
take time to count to ten—ten of your own.

The person who sows seeds of kindness
will have a perpetual harvest.

Don't let anger fester for too long.
Make the first move toward reconciliation.

He who talks to you about others
will talk to others about you.

It's nice to be important,
but it's more important to be nice.

Swallowing pride rarely gives you indigestion.

Many things have been opened by mistake,
but none so frequently as the mouth.

Friendships cemented
together with sin do not hold.

CHARACTER

There's a beautiful body of water in England called Mill Pond, where swans frequently make a stop on their annual migration. Stretched across one corner of the pond are overhead power lines. A number of swans have been killed because they didn't see the power lines as they approached the pond to make a landing. After neighbors complained, the power company installed red flags on the lines. The swans, now alerted to the danger, avoid the lines. Since the red flags were installed, not a single swan has died.

Proverbs are meant to act like those red flags that were provided for the swans' protection. With enough repetition, the Amish principles of simple living should pop into a person's mind when he sees danger ahead. The Amish understand a biblical truth: paths that lead to sin—like those power lines—can be nearly invisible, yet have devastating consequences to one's character.

Maintaining a person's character begins—and continues—with a decision, so these red flags create "advanced decision making." Under pressure, a well-developed character can stand firm and respond by knowing God's way. The best way. Tempted to lie to get out of a tight spot? Up pops the red flag: "The Lord detests lying lips" (Prov. 12:22 NIV). Decision made! Such principles of wisdom have been so engrained through repetitive use of proverbs and sayings that, when one is faced with a critical crossroad in daily life, vital messages trumpet out good judgment.

Easy to remember, proverbs can clarify the difference between right and wrong, good and evil; they help an individual avoid moral mud puddles. With rich and colorful language, these sayings evoke vivid word pictures:

"You can smell scorched soup from afar" is a reminder that gossip spreads like wildfire.

"Much straw but little grain" is a person who is all talk but no substance.

This one needs no explanation: "They who trim themselves to suit others will soon whittle themselves away."

The Amish believe that no one is born with an innately good character . . . and pride is every human being's "default button." It's where our natures tend to slip. Curiously, many common sayings have to do with a mule facing the consequences. . . . of being mulish: "Wherever an ass falleth, there will he never fall again" means you can put a mule in a dilemma only once. Can't you just picture a father trying to teach his son to learn from a mistake and not repeat it?

Here's a favorite: "'One must remember where it comes from,' said the farmer when the mule kicked him." Wouldn't you love to know the story behind that one?

One of the main tasks of the Christian life is to grow out of folly and into wisdom. Wisdom flows from good character. But part of the process of developing a good character involves making mistakes. Many bromides take a tongue-in-cheek approach to life's mishaps.

"Every hen will lay an imperfect egg now and then" implies that accidents happen in the best of families. "Even a clever hen will lay outside the nest" means that everyone makes mistakes.

But a man who doesn't learn from his mistakes?

Well, as the saying goes, "He went through school like the mule through the mill; in at one end and out at the other."

Now *that* is cause for concern.

If you are too big to do little things,
you are probably too little to be
trusted with big things.

Good character like good soup
is usually homemade.

Men think highly of those who rise
rapidly in the world; whereas nothing rises
quicker than dust, straw, and feathers.

Enthusiasm is contagious
and so is the lack of it.

A truly humble person is not easily offended.

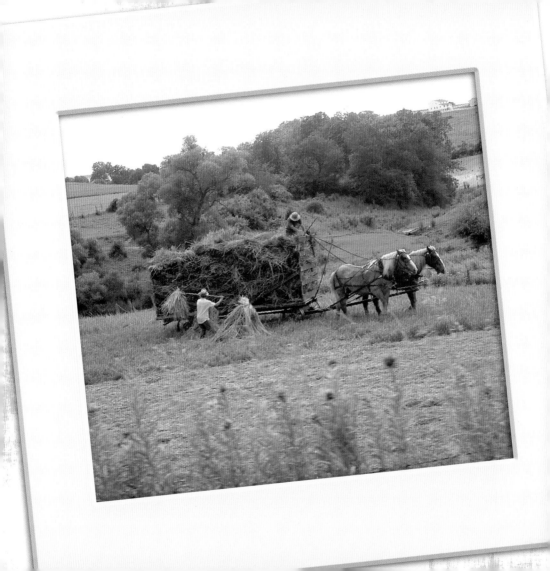

You can tell a man's character
by what he turns up when offered a job—
his nose or his sleeves.

Humility comes from understanding that the
obstacles in front of you will not go away.

You can look a man into the face
but not into the heart.

Fat hens lay few eggs.

He who has never done anything wrong
has never done anything right.

Better to die honest than to live in disgrace.

JUST FOR FUN

If you are under the impression that
the Amish don't have a sense of humor,
well, "have another think" . . .

Every family tree has a little sap.

Age is a question of mind over matter.
If you don't mind, it doesn't matter.

Those who have no children
know best how to raise them.

If the grass looks greener on
the other side, fertilize.

Short hair is quickly brushed.

If you can swallow a pill while drinking from
a water fountain, you deserve to get well.

Kissing wears out, cooking don't.

A woman's work is not seen
unless it's not done.

There is one thing more exasperating
than a wife who can cook and won't,
and that's the wife who can't cook and will.

Conscience: that still, small voice
that makes you even smaller.

Nothing is quite so annoying as to
have someone go right on talking
when you are interrupting.

Don't sell a poor horse near home.

NOTES

Introduction: The Amish in Their Own Words

1. J. Vernon McGee, *Thru the Bible with J. Vernon McGee*, Volume III, Proverbs–Malachi (Nashville: Thomas Nelson, 1982), 1.

2. Edwin Miller Fogel, *Proverbs of the Pennsylvania Germans* (Millersville, PA: Center for Pennsylvania German Studies, 1995), v.

3. E-mail conversation with Dr. Kraybill, Summer 2009.

Time

1. Joe Wittmer, PhD, correspondence with author, Summer 2009.

Money

1. Annenberg Center for the Digital Future at University of Southern California (June 16, 2009) www.digitalcenter.org/pdf/cdf_family _time.pdf.

Children and Family

1. Young Center for Anabaptist and Pietist Studies at Elizabethtown College in Pennsylvania, http://www2.etown.edu/Population_ Trends_2007-2008.asp.

In Word and Deed

1. *The Budget*, (Sugarcreek, OH). Quote reprinted with permission from editor Fannie Erb-Miller.

Work Ethic

1. Philip Rucker, "Bullish on Amish-Built," *The Washington Post*, February 1, 2007, www. washingtonpost.com/wp-dyn/content/ article/2007/01/03/AR2007013101894.

Education

1. Joe Wittmer, PhD, *The Gentle People: An Inside View of Amish Life* (Washington, IN: Black Buggy, 2007), 149.

Suzanne Woods Fisher first became interested in the culture of the Plain People through her grandfather, W. D. Benedict, who was raised in the Old Order German Baptist Brethren Church (also known as Dunkards) in Franklin County, Pennsylvania. She has a warm relationship with her Dunkard cousins and asks them many questions, which they patiently answer.

Suzanne is the author of *Amish Peace: Simple Wisdom for a Complicated World* and the novel *The Choice*, the first book in the *Lancaster County Secrets* series. Her work has appeared in many magazines, including *Today's Christian Woman*, *Worldwide Challenge*, *ParentLife*, *Christian Parenting Today*, *Marriage Partnership*, and many others. Suzanne lives with her family in the San Francisco Bay Area.

Suzanne loves to hear from her readers. Find her online at www.suzannewoodsfisher.com.

Don't miss the new bestselling Amish fiction series

Lancaster County has always been her home—but where does her heart belong?

LANCASTER COUNTY *Secrets*

Sometimes we find love
where we least expect it.

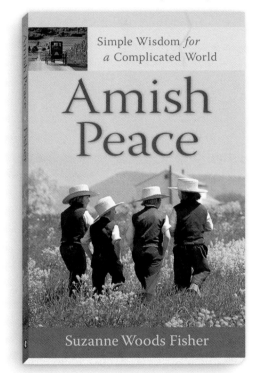